Earw

Barrie Watts

A & C Black · London

Here is an earwig.

Have you ever found an insect like this one? It is an earwig. It lives in dark damp places under stones and logs. Look at the pincers on the end of its body.

Here is a male earwig and a female earwig.

The female is on the right. She has straighter pincers than the male.

This book will tell you how an earwig comes from an egg.

A CIP catalogue record for this book is available from the British Library.

Published by A & C Black (Publishers) Limited
35 Bedford Row, London WC1R 4JH

Acknowledgements
The artwork is by Helen Senior
The publishers would like to thank Michael Chinery for his help and advice.

ISBN 0 7136 3094 9

Filmset by August Filmsetting, Haydock, St Helens
Printed in Belgium by Henri Proost & Cie Pvba

Earwigs eat lots of different foods.

This earwig is eating a daisy petal. Earwigs like to eat lots of different kinds of food. In a garden, they will eat plants like lettuces and cabbages.

Earwigs are good climbers. They will climb apple trees to eat the fruit. They can also fly although they don't often do this.

Look at the drawing.

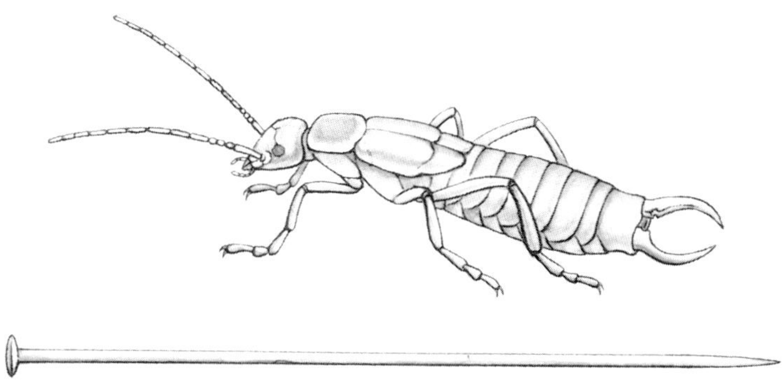

An adult earwig is as big as a pin.

The earwig protects itself.

When the earwig is in danger, it waves its pincers to frighten its enemy, like this.

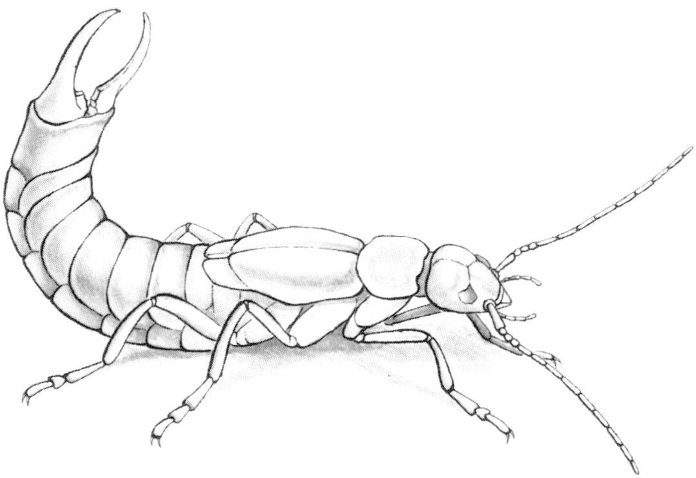

The pincers can give a hard nip.

Look at the big photograph. The earwig's pincers are shown close up. Can you see the joints on the earwig's body? An earwig has a hard skin and the joints help it to bend its body.

The earwigs dig a hole for the winter.

In summer, earwigs hide in dark places during the day. This earwig is hiding in the bark of a log. It will come out at night to eat.

In autumn, the male and female earwig dig a hole under a stone together. They use their jaws to move the earth.

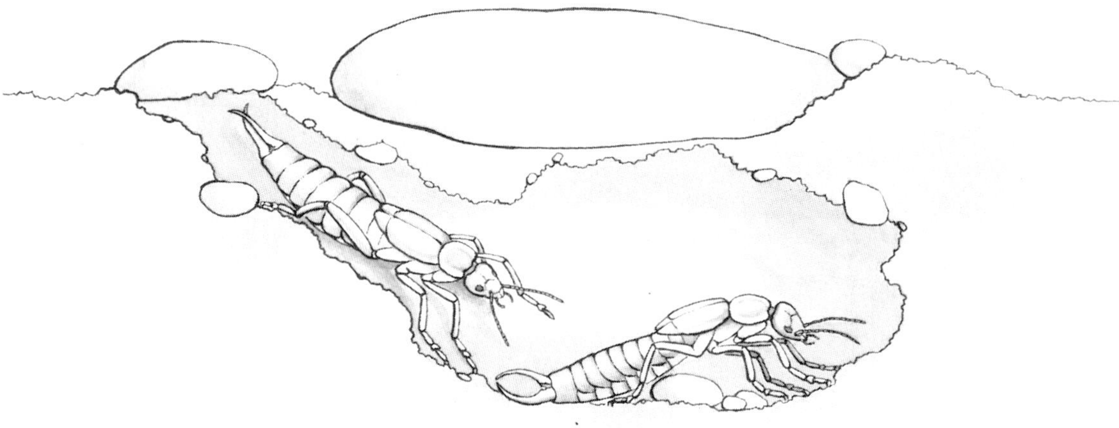

The earwigs will stay in the hole through the winter.

The earwig lays her eggs.

During the winter, the earwigs mate several times.

In spring, the male leaves the hole. Under the ground, the female lays her eggs. She will lay as many as fifty eggs.

Look at the photograph. These eggs are shown very big. In real life, two of these eggs would fit on top of a pin.

The earwig looks after her eggs.

Most insects leave their eggs. The female earwig stays with her eggs to look after them.

These eggs are still soft. They will become harder.

Sometimes a bird or a person digging disturbs the nest and the eggs are scattered. In the big photograph the earwig is collecting her eggs together again. She carefully picks one up in her mouth and takes it back to the nest.

The eggs hatch.

In the nest, the earwig lies on her eggs to keep mites away from them. She keeps the eggs clean by licking them. If they become mouldy, they will not hatch.

After about two weeks, the eggs hatch. The young earwigs are called nymphs.

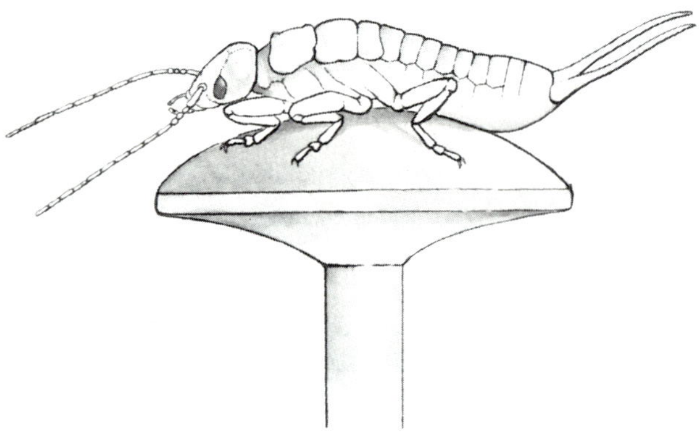

An earwig nymph has a soft white body. It is about as big as the top of a pin.

The young earwigs stay close to their mother.

The female earwig looks after her young and brings them food. If there is danger, she protects them by waving her pincers. Look at the small photograph.

Can you see that some of the eggs have not hatched?

As the nymphs get older, they start to leave their mother. The nymph in the big photograph is looking for food. It still has soft skin and soft pincers. It cannot yet protect itself.

The young earwig grows fast.

The nymph grows quickly. As it gets bigger, its skin gets too tight. Then its skin starts to split, like this:

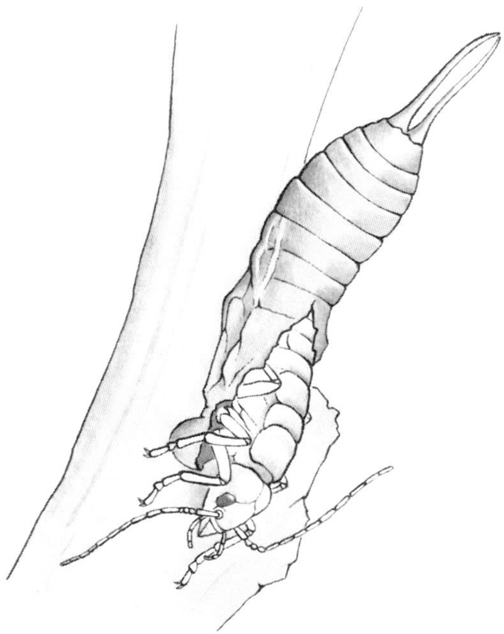

Look at the big photograph. This young earwig has just come out of its old skin. Its new skin is soft and white. The earwig will change its skin three more times before it is fully grown.

The earwig has wings.

Look at the big photograph. This earwig has finished changing its skin. Its old skin lies next to it. The new skin is beginning to get hard and change colour.

In summer, the earwig changes its skin for the last time. It is now fully grown and has wings on its back. This earwig has opened its wings and it will fly away.

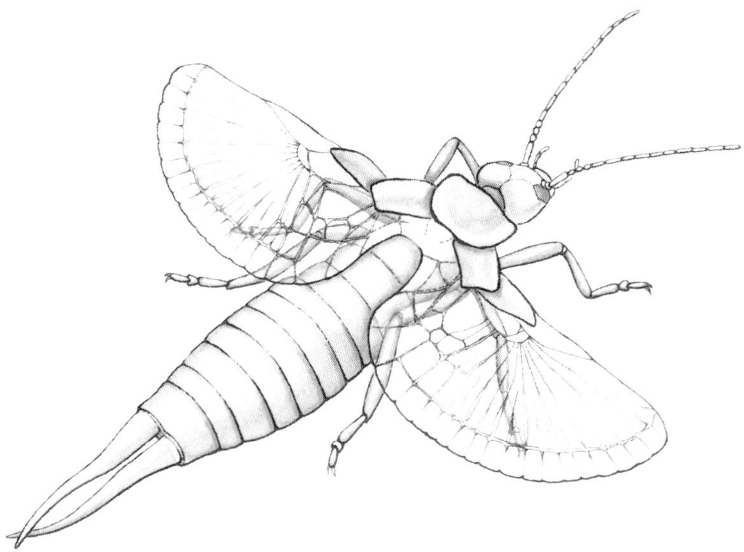

When the earwig stops flying, it uses its pincers to fold its wings up very small and tuck them under its wing cases.

The earwig is fully grown.

At the end of the summer, the earwig looks for a place to spend the winter.

When she finds a mate, they will dig a nest under the log.

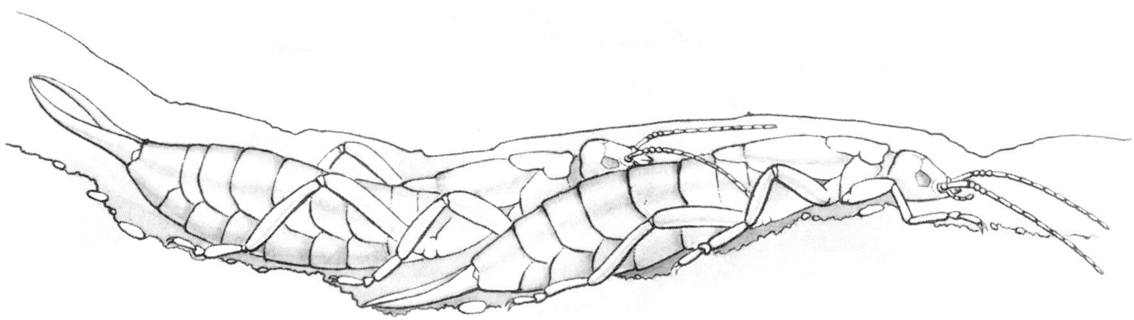

In winter, they will mate.

What do you think will happen then?

Do you remember how an earwig came from an egg?
See if you can tell the story in your own words.
You can use these pictures to help you.

1

→

2

→

4

→

5

→

3

6

Try to find and watch some earwigs.
See if you can find a female and her young.

Index

This index will help you to find some of the important words in this book.